KEN ANDERSON, JAMES BROOKS, PETE JOHNSON, CARL PICKENS, CHAD JOHNSON, BOB TRUMPY, ANTHONY MUNOZ, WILLIE ANDERSON, MAX MONTOYA, BRUCE REIMERS, BOB JOHNSON, EDDIE EDWARDS, ROSS BROWNER, TIM KRUMRIE, MIKE REID, REGGIE WILLIAMS, BRIAN SIMMONS, JAMES FRANCIS,

THE STORY OF THE CINCINNATI BENGALS

KEN RILEY, LEMAR PARRISH, DAVID FULCHER, SOLOMON WILCOTS, SHAYNE GRAHAM, LEE JOHNSON, KEN ANDERSON, JAMES BROOKS, PETE JOHNSON, CARL PICKENS, CHAD JOHNSON, BOB TRUMPY,

THE STORY OF THE
CINCINNATI BENGALS

BY JIM WHITING

CREATIVE EDUCATION / CREATIVE PAPERBACKS

PUBLISHED BY CREATIVE EDUCATION AND CREATIVE PAPERBACKS
P.O. BOX 227, MANKATO, MINNESOTA 56002
CREATIVE EDUCATION AND CREATIVE PAPERBACKS ARE IMPRINTS OF THE
CREATIVE COMPANY
WWW.THECREATIVECOMPANY.US

DESIGN AND PRODUCTION BY BLUE DESIGN (WWW.BLUEDES.COM)
ART DIRECTION BY RITA MARSHALL
PRINTED IN CHINA

PHOTOGRAPHS BY CORBIS (MICHAEL KEATING/AP), GETTY IMAGES (PETER
AIKEN/STRINGER, SYLVIA ALLEN/NFL, SCOTT BOEHM, CLIFTON BOUTELLE/
NFL, PETER BROUILLET/NFL, ROB BROWN, KEVIN C. COX, DIAMOND IMAGES,
GIN ELLIS, ELSA, GEORGE GOJKOVICH, SAM GREENWOOD, JOHN GRIESHOP/
STRINGER, ANDY LYONS, WALLY MCNAMEE/CORBIS, AL MESSERSCHMIDT,
DONALD MIRALLE, NFL, JOE ROBBINS, GEORGE ROSE, MANNY RUBIO/NFL,
DILIP VISHWANAT, HARRY E. WALKER/MCT)

NAMES: WHITING, JIM, AUTHOR.
TITLE: THE STORY OF THE CINCINNATI BENGALS / JIM WHITING.
SERIES: NFL TODAY.
INCLUDES INDEX.
SUMMARY: THIS HIGH-INTEREST HISTORY OF THE NATIONAL FOOTBALL
LEAGUE'S CINCINNATI BENGALS HIGHLIGHTS MEMORABLE GAMES, SUMMARIZES
SEASONAL TRIUMPHS AND DEFEATS, AND FEATURES STANDOUT PLAYERS SUCH
AS ANDY DALTON.
IDENTIFIERS: LCCN 2018035581 / ISBN 978-1-64026-136-5 (HARDCOVER) / ISBN
978-1-62832-699-4 (PBK) / ISBN 978-1-64000-254-8 (EBOOK)
SUBJECTS: LCSH: CINCINNATI BENGALS (FOOTBALL TEAM)—HISTORY—
JUVENILE LITERATURE.
CLASSIFICATION: LCC GV956.C6 W4698 2019 / DDC 796.332/640977178—DC23

FIRST EDITION HC 9 8 7 6 5 4 3 2 1
FIRST EDITION PBK 9 8 7 6 5 4 3 2 1

COVER: A.J. GREEN
PAGE 2: JOE MIXON
PAGES 6-7: GREG COOK

TABLE OF CONTENTS

GRIDIRON GREATS

COMING IN FROM THE COLD

For Cincinnati Bengals coach Forrest Gregg, history was repeating itself. On December 31, 1967, he had played in the National Football League (NFL) Championship. At the start of the game, the temperature was -13 °F (-25 °C). The windchill made it feel like -23 °F (-30.6 °C). It got colder as the game went on. People dubbed it the "Ice Bowl." Gregg was right tackle for the Green Bay Packers. They trailed the Dallas Cowboys with 16 seconds left. Gregg helped open a gap in the Dallas defensive line. It was just wide enough for quarterback Bart Starr to dive into the end zone. That gave the Packers a 21–17 win.

CINCINNATI BENGALS

Fourteen years later, Gregg's team was playing in what would become known as the "Freezer Bowl." The temperature in Cincinnati was -9 °F (-22.8 °C). The windchill dropped to -32 °F (-35.6 °C). The Bengals faced the San Diego Chargers for the American Football Conference (AFC) championship. The winner would advance to Super Bowl XVI. Conditions were bad. The Chargers' owner wanted to postpone the game. The Bengals said no. They felt the frigid weather would ground San Diego's powerful passing attack.

Gregg had prepared his players for the cold. They practiced outside for several days beforehand. Guard Dave Lapham said, "Forrest said it was going to be like going to the dentist. You weren't going to like it, but you had to do it, so let's just concentrate on getting through it." San Diego had a different way of preparing. "The Chargers were coming from California," added cornerback Ken Riley. "We heard they showed up for practice Saturday and got right back on the bus to go back to the hotel."

LEFT: BENGALS MASCOT

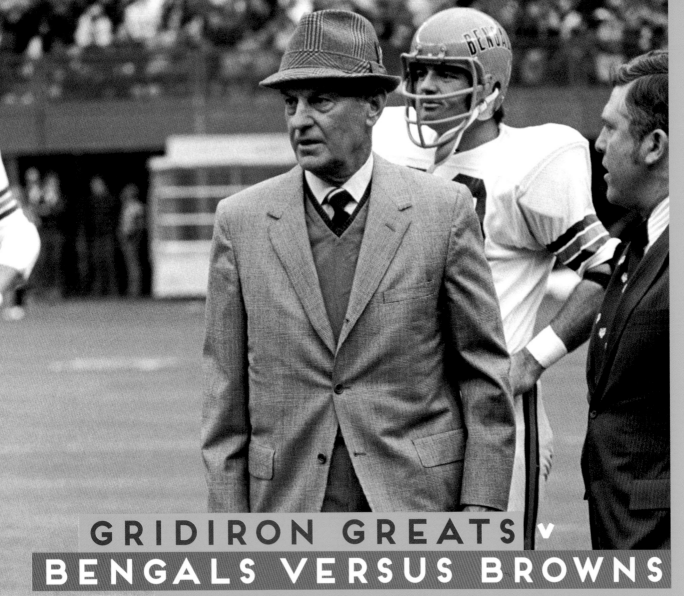

GRIDIRON GREATS v
BENGALS VERSUS BROWNS

The Cincinnati Bengals and Cleveland Browns both have ties to Paul Brown. He founded and coached each Ohio team. Now they are natural rivals. They are in the same division and play each other regularly. One famous incident occurred when the teams weren't playing each other, though. In December 1989, the Bengals hosted the Seahawks. Bengals fans pelted referees with snowballs after some questionable calls. Cincinnati coach Sam Wyche picked up a microphone. "Will the next person that sees anybody throw anything onto this field point them out and get them out of here?" he bellowed. "You don't live in Cleveland—you live in Cincinnati!" His scolding worked. The snowball storm stopped.

RUNNING BACK PETE JOHNSON

"FORREST SAID IT WAS GOING TO BE LIKE GOING TO THE DENTIST. YOU WEREN'T GOING TO LIKE IT, BUT YOU HAD TO DO IT."

—DAVE LAPHAM ON THE FREEZER BOWL

The Bengals' linemen wanted to intimidate the Chargers. They didn't wear sleeves under their jerseys. Their arms were bare. Several Bengals wore pantyhose to help them stay warm. Defensive end Eddie Edwards wore a heated cap on the sideline. It was a mistake. His ears were burned. But that was about all that went wrong for the Bengals. They took an early 10–0 lead. San Diego turned the ball over four times. Cincinnati quarterback Ken Anderson completed 14 of 22 passes. Two went for touchdowns. The Bengals went on to win, 27–7.

When the game ended, Gregg was on the winning side in the two coldest games in NFL history. "What I'll always remember is how our guys played like it was another game," he said. "They just went to work like it was any other day. And the way they executed in those conditions was just amazing."

ANTHONY MUÑOZ
OFFENSIVE TACKLE

BENGALS SEASONS: 1980–92
HEIGHT: 6-FOOT-6
WEIGHT: 278 POUNDS

GRIDIRON GREATS ˅

BIG RISK, BIG REWARD

The Bengals had the third overall pick in the 1980 NFL Draft. With it, they selected offensive tackle Anthony Muñoz. Many people thought it was a huge risk. The mountainous Muñoz was plagued by knee problems in college. But the risk paid off. Muñoz became a starter as a rookie. He anchored the offensive line for 13 seasons. He was selected for the Pro Bowl 11 times. His size gave him an advantage in blocking opposing defenders. His quick feet and sure hands made him a solid receiver as well. He nabbed seven passes for four touchdowns in his career.

185

185 GAMES PLAYED

11 PRO BOWL APPEARANCES

BUILDING THE BENGALS

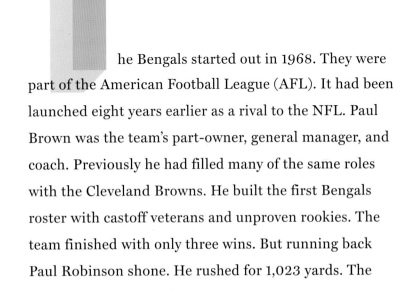

The Bengals started out in 1968. They were part of the American Football League (AFL). It had been launched eight years earlier as a rival to the NFL. Paul Brown was the team's part-owner, general manager, and coach. Previously he had filled many of the same roles with the Cleveland Browns. He built the first Bengals roster with castoff veterans and unproven rookies. The team finished with only three wins. But running back Paul Robinson shone. He rushed for 1,023 yards. The

254

254 CAREER TOUCHDOWNS

187

187 GAMES PLAYED

**BOOMER ESIASON
QUARTERBACK**

BENGALS SEASONS: 1984-92, 1997
HEIGHT: 6-FOOT-5
WEIGHT: 224 POUNDS

GRIDIRON GREATS ᵛ
GETTING A KICK OUT OF BOOMER

Norman Julius Esiason kicked a lot in his mother's womb. Before he was even born, she called him Boomer. The nickname stuck. It became one of the most recognizable names in pro football. His powerful arm propelled the Bengals to their second Super Bowl appearance. That year, he earned the league's Most Valuable Player (MVP) award. He set several NFL passing records for left-handed quarterbacks. He was also surprisingly mobile. He rushed for almost 1,600 yards during his career. In 1995, he was named Walter Payton NFL Man of the Year. Today, he is a popular broadcaster.

CINCINNATI BENGALS

performance earned him Rookie of the Year honors. The AFL merged with the NFL in 1970. That year, the Bengals improved to 8–6. This record sent them on their first trip to the playoffs. They lost in the first round to the Baltimore Colts. But the Bengals had tasted success. They were eager for more.

In 1973, they got another chance. Anderson was quarterback. Speedy Essex Johnson ran the ball. Sure-handed rookie receiver Isaac Curtis raced down the field. The Bengals won 10 games. They returned to the playoffs. But the Miami Dolphins beat them in the first round. By then, Anderson was one of the finest passers in football. His favorite targets were Curtis and tight end Bob Trumpy. The Bengals finished with an impressive 11–3 record in 1975. They marched to their third playoff appearance. Again, they lost in the first round.

In 1981, Anderson set new team records. He had 3,754 passing yards and 29 touchdown passes that season. Linebacker Reggie Williams led a stingy defense. Rookie receiver Cris Collinsworth added energy to the offense. Cincinnati won 12 games. It roared back to the playoffs. The Bengals toppled the Buffalo Bills. It was their first-ever playoff win. Their hot streak continued in the Freezer Bowl. There, they beat San Diego. This placed them in Super Bowl XVI. They faced the San Francisco 49ers.

CINCINNATI BENGALS

"EVERYBODY IN CINCINNATI IS PROUD OF YOU, AND YOU SHOULD TAKE PRIDE IN YOURSELVES."

—COACH FORREST GREGG

Cincinnati got off to a bumpy start. In the first half alone, the team had three turnovers. Legendary 49ers quarterback Joe Montana took advantage of the Bengals' mistakes. He guided his team to a 20–0 halftime lead. The Bengals scored a touchdown early in the third quarter. They added another in the fourth quarter. But the Niners responded with a pair of field goals. With 16 seconds left, Anderson's touchdown pass narrowed the score to 26–21. But San Francisco recovered an onside kick. The game was over. Afterward, Gregg consoled his players. "You guys played one heck of a second half," he told them. "Everybody in Cincinnati is proud of you, and you should take pride in yourselves."

KEN ANDERSON

SHUFFLING TO THE SUPER BOWL

PAUL BROWN STADIUM

A players' strike shortened the 1982 season. The Bengals' 7–2 record sent them to the playoffs again. But the New York Jets quickly eliminated them. Then the offense sputtered. The 1983 season started with six losses in the first seven weeks. It ended with a 7–9 record. The Bengals drafted lefty quarterback Boomer Esiason in 1984. The plan was to groom him to replace Anderson. Esiason's arm was like a cannon. He had a healthy dose of confidence, too.

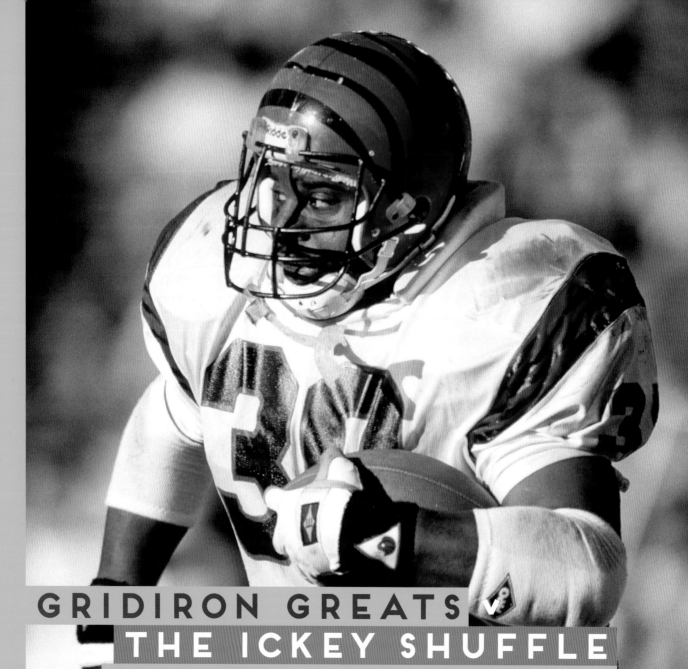

GRIDIRON GREATS
THE ICKEY SHUFFLE

Rookie running back Elbert "Ickey" Woods scored 15 touchdowns in 1988. Fans loved his end zone dance. He faced the crowd. He stretched his arms out wide. Then he hopped twice to the left. Next, he hopped twice to the right and spiked the ball. Finally, he twirled his right index finger over his head while swiveling his hips and shouting, "Woo! Woo! Woo!" Local media dubbed it the "Ickey Shuffle." It was replicated by teammates and fans alike. Even owner Paul Brown, who was 80 at the time, did it. The dance sparked songs, shirts, commercials, and an Ickey milkshake.

27

27 CAREER TOUCHDOWNS

37

37 GAMES PLAYED

He got his first start early in the season. Anderson was injured. "I don't expect to throw five touchdown passes," he told reporters before the game, "but I also don't expect to throw five interceptions." Neither happened. Esiason scored the game's only touchdown on a short run. The Bengals defeated the Houston Oilers, 13–3.

Esiason took over as the starting quarterback in 1985. He threw for 3,443 yards and 27 touchdowns. He was protected by a strong offensive line. It was anchored by Anthony Muñoz. The Bengals improved to 10–6 in 1986. But it was not good enough for the playoffs.

Two years later, the Bengals clawed their way to 12 wins. A big factor was rookie running back Ickey Woods. He led Cincinnati with 1,066 rushing yards. He had 15 touchdowns. After each one, he entertained fans with a dance. It was called the "Ickey Shuffle." Woods and his teammates shuffled through the playoffs. First they celebrated a 21–13 victory over the Seattle Seahawks. Then they added a 21–10 win against the Bills. All that remained

ICKEY WOODS (WHO ALSO WORE NUMBER 30)

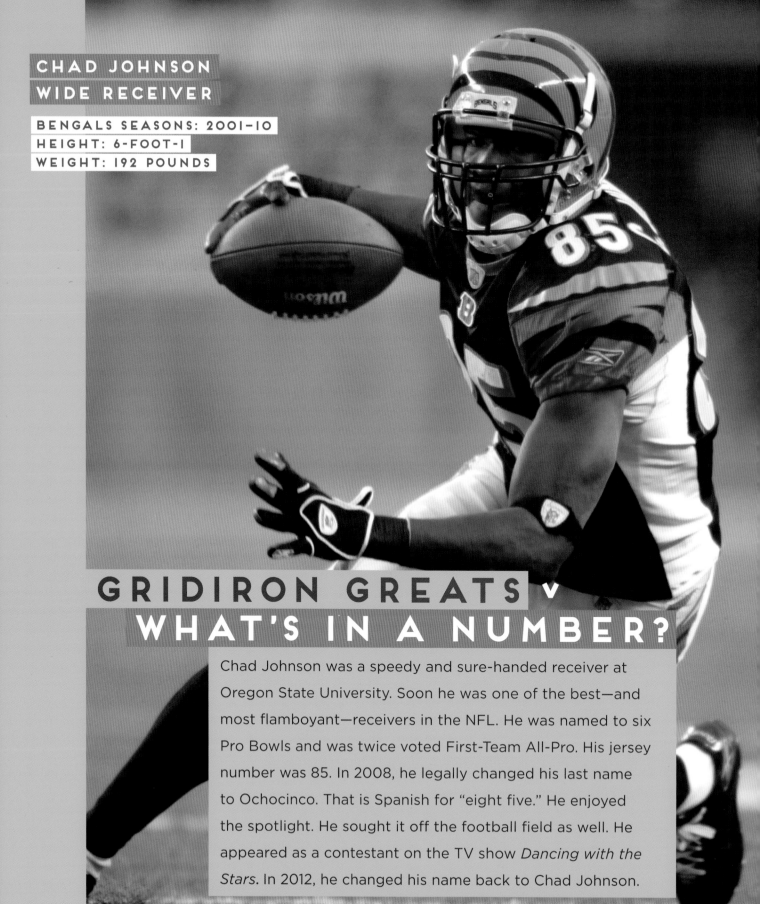

CHAD JOHNSON
WIDE RECEIVER

BENGALS SEASONS: 2001–10
HEIGHT: 6-FOOT-1
WEIGHT: 192 POUNDS

GRIDIRON GREATS
WHAT'S IN A NUMBER?

Chad Johnson was a speedy and sure-handed receiver at Oregon State University. Soon he was one of the best—and most flamboyant—receivers in the NFL. He was named to six Pro Bowls and was twice voted First-Team All-Pro. His jersey number was 85. In 2008, he legally changed his last name to Ochocinco. That is Spanish for "eight five." He enjoyed the spotlight. He sought it off the football field as well. He appeared as a contestant on the TV show *Dancing with the Stars*. In 2012, he changed his name back to Chad Johnson.

67

67 CAREER TOUCHDOWNS

166

166 GAMES PLAYED

was Super Bowl XXIII. The Bengals once again met the 49ers in the title game. But there would be no dancing for Woods in the Super Bowl. The Bengals' offense struggled. Cincinnati rebounded in the second half to take the lead. But 49ers quarterback Joe Montana broke their hearts. He completed a last-minute touchdown pass. San Francisco won, 20–16. "It's very disappointing," Esiason said. "We were 34 seconds away from a great victory."

Injuries plagued the Bengals in 1989. The team finished at 8–8. It did not make the playoffs. Cincinnati's 9–7 record in 1990 earned it a spot in the Wild Card round of the playoffs. The Bengals crushed the Houston Oilers, 41–14. But the Los Angeles Raiders ended Cincinnati's run a week later.

THE BUNGLES

Deflated, the Bengals struggled through 1991 and 1992. Esiason threw more interceptions than touchdowns. Cincinnati traded him to the Jets. Still, the team floundered. It endured one losing season after another. The 14-year streak included two 4–12 records and four at 3–13. The Bengals won just two games in 2002. Unfortunately, several draft choices didn't pan out as the team had hoped. A Pittsburgh broadcaster added to the team's misery when he nicknamed them "The Bungles."

Fans found a ray of hope in the midst of the team's losing streak. Esiason returned as a backup quarterback in 1997. The team struggled to 3–8 during the first part of the season. Esiason was back in the pocket for the final five games. Cincinnati won four of them. Bruising rookie running back Corey Dillon complemented Esiason. He ran for 1,129 yards and 10 touchdowns. Esiason ended his career in the best possible fashion. His final pass was a 77-

yard, game-winning touchdown. The team pleaded with him to stay. But he retired.

By 2003, more than half of the players were new. Following its 2002 performance, Cincinnati received the first overall pick in the NFL Draft. With it, the team chose Carson Palmer. He was a strong-armed quarterback. Palmer spent his first season learning from veteran Jon Kitna. Palmer's development was part of the long-term plan for the Bengals' improvement. Meanwhile, Kitna had a sensational year. He connected with flashy wide receiver Chad Johnson for 1,355 of his total 3,591 passing yards. Kitna was the NFL's Comeback Player of the Year. The Bengals finished 8–8 and out of the cellar in the AFC North Division. "It was a good year," said coach Marvin Lewis. "Not a great year—a good year." In 2004, Palmer took over. He threw for 2,897 yards and 18 touchdowns. Rudi Johnson ran for 1,454 yards. Cornerback Tory James snagged eight interceptions. The Bengals finished 8–8 again.

In 2005, the Bengals finally rewarded their fans. They ended the season with the division title and an 11–5 record. Palmer led the league with 32 touchdown passes. Cincinnati was in the playoffs. It was the first time in 15 years! But the team didn't get far. Palmer suffered a severe knee injury on his first pass of the Wild Card game against Pittsburgh. The Steelers won the game, 31–17.

Some experts thought Palmer's injury would end his career. But he made an amazing comeback in 2006. That

year, he set a new team record with 4,035 passing yards.
T. J. Houshmandzadeh and Chad Johnson each recorded
more than 1,000 receiving yards. Going into the final
game of the season, the Bengals had a shot at claiming
a spot in the playoffs. But their hopes were dashed. The
Steelers pulled off a 23–17 overtime victory. In 2007,
Palmer performed even better. But Cincinnati dropped to
7–9. Palmer missed most of the next season with an elbow
injury. The Bengals muddled through with only four wins.

T. J. HOUSHMANDZADEH

ROARING BACK

Palmer returned for the 2009 season opener. The Bengals lost to the Denver Broncos. Then the team went on a tear. It won seven of its next eight games. The Bengals swept all six games against AFC North opponents. At 10–6, Cincinnati found itself atop the division. It was back in the playoffs. The Bengals faced the Jets in the Wild Card. Cincinnati took an early lead. But Palmer threw an interception. Cincinnati missed two field goals. Such sloppy play let the Jets come back and win, 24–14.

The loss put Cincinnati in the NFL record books. The Bengals had endured the most consecutive years—19—without a playoff win. Still,

CINCINNATI BENGALS

41

GRIDIRON GREATS
NO MYSTERY HERE

A famous Sherlock Holmes story is "The Red-Headed League." If there were such a thing in football, Andy Dalton would be its leader. His bright red hair is evident every time he takes off his helmet. Often, he makes his opponents see red. His last-minute touchdown pass in 2017 won the season's final game. It also knocked the Baltimore Ravens out of the playoffs. The Bills squeezed into the playoffs as a result, which made Dalton a hero in Buffalo (temporarily). He became the Bengals' starting quarterback as a rookie and began working his way up the rankings for the team's all-time passing records.

ANDY DALTON
QUARTERBACK

BENGALS SEASONS: 2011-PRESENT
HEIGHT: 6-FOOT-2
WEIGHT: 220 POUNDS

CINCINNATI BENGALS

they kept their hopes high for the 2010 season. Fans were especially excited when electrifying wide receiver Terrell Owens joined the team. At the time, Owens was third all-time among NFL players for receiving yards. Fans thought he would give the offense another powerful weapon. But he couldn't help Cincinnati break a 10-game losing streak. With just four wins, the Bengals plunged back to the bottom of their division. Palmer left at the end of the season. Owens retired.

A pair of rookies boosted the Bengals back into the postseason in 2011. They were quarterback Andy Dalton and wide receiver A. J. Green. Cincinnati finished at 9–7. Again, the Bengals lost in the Wild Card round. But the improvement gave fans a reason to look forward to 2012. The Bengals again qualified for the playoffs. But the Houston Texans shut down the Bengals' offense. The next three years fueled their playoff frustration. The Bengals continued to enjoy winning seasons. But they came up short each time in the postseason.

The 2015 season was especially disheartening. Cincinnati's 12–4 record gave the team the AFC North title. Cincinnati engaged in a bitter defensive battle with Pittsburgh in the Wild Card round. The Bengals trailed 15–0 in the fourth quarter. But they rallied to take a 16–15 lead with less than two minutes remaining. An interception deep in Pittsburgh territory seemed to seal the win. Fans thought Cincinnati had captured its first

LEFT: RUNNING BACK BENJARVUS GREEN-ELLIS

DEFENSIVE TACKLE GENO ATKINS

playoff victory since 1990. But there was a fumble on the next play. The ball went back to Pittsburgh. The Steelers drove downfield. They kicked the winning field goal with 18 seconds left. "This locker room should feel a lot different right now," Dalton said. "We won that game and then we didn't." In 2016, the team went 6–9–1. It missed the playoffs for the first time in six years. Cincinnati won just seven games the following season.

The Bengals have had their share of disappointments. As of 2018, they hadn't won a playoff game since 1990. Yet they keep giving fans reasons to hope for better years to come. Those fans believe that someday soon, the Bengals will leave their bungling ways behind and be known as champions instead.

AFC CHAMPIONSHIPS

1981
1988

CINCINNATI BENGALS

https://www.bengals.com/

NFL: CINCINNATI BENGALS TEAM PAGE

http://www.nfl.com/teams/cincinnatibengals/profile?team=CIN

CINCINNATI BENGALS

INDEX

RUDI JOHNSON